Author Biography

Hester lives in Cape Town, South Africa with her husband William and their three children. She's a long time business owner and has been a greyscale coloring book publisher for a year. Her hobbies are doing all kinds of arts & crafts , photography, reading, gardening, traveling and coloring.

Hester started adult coloring almost three years ago, like most colorists she started with Indie Art (line art) designs and collected a large range of these coloring books. She also support some Indie artists financially through Patreon.

About two years ago the first greyscale artist asked Hester to color her greyscale designs and this is where her love for coloring realy took off. In a matter of months she colored for seven artists, this turn her into an avid colorist. After about a year she started collecting artwork and photographs to come up with her own greyscale coloring book range where the first books she launched were her Fantasy series. In no time the demand for her work grew and now she has her own Facebook coloring group and also her own coloring design team.

Other Titles by the author

Made in the USA
Monee, IL
20 January 2021